The Strategy of Brilliance
A Business Philosophy

By:
Benny R. Ferguson Jr.

The Strategy of Brilliance
By Benny R. Ferguson Jr. © 2018

ISBN – 13: 978-0692433775

Published by:
The Ferguson Company

Editor & cover design:
http://roxanec.wix.com/time-to-read.com

Introduction

In business there is a misconception that has altered the landscape of success. The battle field is fraught with fallen warriors, skilled practitioners of their craft, who have lost their way because of a simple concept.

They measured their success against others who may have been, instead of against their own "Ideal." They focused on the money, the financial return instead of focusing on the conditions that would yield that financial return.

Although both are important, we are going to delve into an understanding of business that has been lost. We are going to explore into a subjective, mental aspect of business and how it is done, how it is approached, that automatically places you in alignment with the financial rewards, the social rewards, and the intrinsic rewards that a service to humanity yields.

We are going to look at the major areas that drive business ultimately to its success or failure, which are leadership, culture, customer service, and sales. Within these areas, the necessary mental landscape to command performance, production, and the realization of potential, also aligns you and your business with your highest goals and objectives.

You must connect yourself to these ideas, and make them your natural way of operating on a daily basis. If you add them to your skill set, you will find that you become congruent in your inner mental activity and your outward physical activity, and that the results you get become much more profound because you have become a beacon of laser focus.

I'm excited that you are reading this material, that you are a seeker of possibility, looking for the edge, the final piece to the puzzle, and here you will find it. To know your sole place of control and to begin placing your efforts there sets you quantum leaps above and beyond your competition.

Cheers to your success, and the inevitable fulfillment of your happiness.

Benny R. Ferguson Jr.

Leadership

The Air Around You

As a leader, it is imperative to evaluate the air around you constantly. What vibration are you giving off? Is the energy, the emotion, the character, the personality that is you, creating an air that builds and allows those around you to excel?

A true leader develops those around him/her and then allows them to shine in their position. The janitor, the secretary, to your most prized employee or partner, once competent in their position should receive the material and emotional support from you, the leader, that allows them to take their tools and gifts to the next level. In the grand scheme of life, it is those who have had great models, great leadership, that often become great leaders, and if that position has fallen to your shoulders it is a grand responsibility.

It is your responsibility to groom them. It is your responsibility to coach them in managing life *outside* the work environment so that it does not affect performance *inside* the work environment. It is your responsibility to be a source of solidarity and consistency for those closest to you. In short show them how it is done.

Are you approachable? Do your key people feel comfortable approaching you with their challenges? Do you truly listen, or do you offer advice without all the facts and without taking into consideration the emotional aspects of those involved? Are you seen as a part of the team, or have you positioned yourself figuratively above them?

All of these can serve to hinder or catapult performance, and you must be mindful of how these are being perceived by your team.

Communicate Systematically

Communication is the area that most often has the greatest breakdowns in organizations. It is also, what you might call the silent killer, because unlike bad behaviors, which are obvious and visible in nature, a lack of, or broken communication's effects, cannot often be seen and are not obvious until it has reached a critically detrimental point.

Communication is greatest when it is free, and individuals are equipped with the tools to speak of their needs and state their position without worry of retaliation or blame. Communication is greatest when leadership reveals its ability to make mistakes, and that mistakes are a key to growth. Communication is greatest when all parties strive to resolve issues quickly for the good of the team.

The stage for this level of communication and behavior is and must be set by leadership. It cannot and will not simply fall into place by those with good intentions. It must be guided, directed, and modeled in a way that is visible and understandable by the team as to what and how the behavior of communication is expected to be displayed.

Trust and *absolute confidence* are needed when we speak of this level of communication. It is imperative that the intangibles of high levels of character be present when communication is to be at its highest level, at a level that fosters relationship, high performance, production, and the realization of limitless potential. Individuals must feel free to express themselves in the proper light, in their space, to feel empowered to create a new masterpiece of performance each and every day.

Now, am I going to list each and every characteristic of this level of communication for you? No. True empowerment comes from helping you to realize that you are the commander, and that when you begin to build the "Ideal" in your mind, you begin to draw or attract its attributes to you, and when the necessary facets of this level of communication comes through to you and your team, you own it. There is no time frame to try integrating it into behavior or allowing buy-in from everyone, especially if everyone participated in its creation.

Listen Intently

An incredibly important facet of leadership is the ability to listen intently. Direct reports can be empowered or disempowered by the simple fact of whether they feel that leadership actually listens to their concerns.

Validating the ideas, the challenges outside of the job, and potential career changing decisions serves to solidify the relationship that you forge with your team and the magnitude of the effort that they will put forth for you in their day to day activities.

To listen intently is to make time for communication to take place. It does not have to be at random, especially the larger the organization, but even in that arena it should be scheduled. It should be scheduled so that you as the leader always have an idea of the concerns, the triumphs, the losses and the failures that are affecting the performance of your team.

What does it mean to listen intently? Are you good at it at this moment? What would your family, your friends, your colleagues, your team say? If you do not need their feedback, begin to develop the idea of what it looks like to listen intently in your mind, to be present, not to think about a million other things while someone is communicating to you. It is the ultimate sign of respect to be present. To know, to understand, to grasp what is being said by those closest to you is vital. It is the only sure way to keep your fingers on the pulse of your team and organization.

Inspire Intrinsically

There is nothing more powerful than inwardly motivated individuals, individuals who are driven by their own personal cause, whether it is to save the world or simply to satisfy an insatiable hunger to be the best. Which one is driving you? Personal performance is a byproduct of the forces at work on the inside of a person, so let's look at a few of the norms.

Fear is most often the driver. The fear of being broke, the fear of losing a job, the fear of losing respect; and these drivers are often established when a person is young, so they continue to use them for themselves and to impose them on others. Although fear can be a powerful motivator, it carries consequences.

1. When the situation that causes the fear is satisfied, the motivation is gone, and therefore a new fear must be instituted.
2. Fear is not a precursor to relationship. Fear is a destroyer of relationship. It breeds resentment, jealousy, frustration, and stress; and these are great for relationship, right? No!

Now on the flip side of the coin, establishing intrinsic motivation, a motivation that appeals to a person's self-interest, is much more powerful. What are the members of your team or organization looking for? What are they trying to accomplish in their lives? How is working with you going to help them move forward and up in a way that inspires, motivates, and simultaneously helps you accomplish your goals as a leader? When people feel that they are on track to reach their personal goals, and that you are helping them do it, they have no problem going to war with you to help you accomplish your goals in the process.

Find the internal motivation of your people, that motivation that drives them to excel without any extra effort from you, and watch them perform.

It's Important To You

What is important to you? Just as your life is an exact reflection of who you are on the inside; your business, your organization, your department, and your team is also a direct and perfect reflection of who you are.

As a leader, how well do you communicate all necessary information to your team? How well do you listen to the concerns of others? Do you stick to established protocols, or do you allow others to break the rules just as you do? What type of energy do you bring to the work environment on a daily basis? Is it swayed by situations and circumstances outside of the team, or do you focus on setting the example for everyone who looks to you for guidance and direction? Are the lines of communication open to you? Does your team feel free to express themselves; to make comments and suggestions about what they believe will improve the overall performance of the team or improve service and relations with customer or clients?

Everything that is important to you will be important to your team. The behaviors that you display will be displayed within your team. Leaders must become acutely aware of their behaviors and the implicit impact that they have on the culture and the performance of the team. A leader is the one who sets the tone and all the parameters within the team. High performance or the lack of performance is the result of the type of environment that the leader has allowed, or has consciously set in place.

They Are Important To You

To what extent is your team important to you? Do they feel the excitement you have for them, and the honor that is yours to have them working by your side? Do they know how much you appreciate their efforts, their commitment to excellence, and their support of the team as a whole? Do they know how much you care for their well-being, and that you support them in their dealings with extended family as well as within the work family?

Yes, family.

Do your suppliers and vendors know how important they are to you?

Whether you can replace them next week or not, it still needs to be mentioned that the individuals who grace your company grounds as vendors or suppliers should be seen as important to you as well. These individuals also represent a voice that can communicate pleasant behavior or ill-will about your company to the public at large. As a leader, do you make them a part of the team? Are they comfortable expressing themselves to you? If your direct team members were your children, the individuals that represent your vendors and suppliers are your cousins. Treat them as family, and become aware of the benefits that this heightened level of relationship brings.

Painting The Picture

It is not enough merely to be the model and example of what you want your business, your organization, your department, or your team to look like, although it must be done first. You must also begin to paint the picture in the minds of your team members. This is how you override preconceived notions and ideas that team members may be bringing into the work environment.

As a leader, you have mental images of what a high performing team looks like. You have images of what excellence looks like. You must make it a priority and a practice to sow these images into your team members.

"I can see you being a fantastic addition to the team."
"We, as a department excel at the quality of work we produce."
"We, as an organization carry a magnificent reputation within the community."

Whatever the highest goals and objectives, whatever the supporting behaviors and mindsets, once you, as the leader, have outlined all that is necessary, you must begin to sow those images into your team. Once the images are burned into the minds of your team through repetition, the associated behaviors will begin to manifest unconsciously and become the norm rather than the exception. But, you as the leader must go first, otherwise you will not be able to

11

convey the message consistently and sow the images for the type and level of performance and production you desire.

Spelling It Out

The vision that you have for yourself and your team comes with no small level of importance. The truth of the matter is that it is the most important thing. It is the vehicle that calls or brings to light all of the requirements for success. It is also the light that reveals all areas of deficiency. When you have a specifically outlined vision, a vision that is a clear image within the mind, and you begin to convey/sow that image within yourself and your team, it becomes obvious whether the requisite behaviors are present to support the level of performance and production required to fulfill and achieve the vision.

At the outset individuals are reluctant to change because it often requires growth. It requires new ways of thinking and feeling, higher mental and emotional states. It requires an acute conscious awareness of oneself in order to reverse your direction as soon as you realize that you are not behaving in ways that are conducive to the level of performance and production required by the new vision that is being sewn.

It is also a matter of focus. Gone are the days of concerning ourselves with the shortcomings of others. What they said, what they did, how they offended, why they were late, what they should and should not be doing. If everyone is being enlisted to be a leader, and this is the new norm, then the focus should now be set squarely on ourselves as individual players on the team, and how can I make sure that I am thinking, feeling, behaving, performing, and producing, BRILLIANTLY, in a manner that is projecting me, my team, my department, my organization toward its highest goals and objectives, towards the current vision that is now being sewn.

But I reiterate that this new philosophy is not one to be passed down through the ranks as something that everyone else should go and do. It is imperative that you as the leader, no matter where you are in the organization, go first. You must be the model, the example. You do not spell it out with your words in the company newsletter or over interoffice emails. You spell it out in your behaviors. You spell it out starting with your new thought patterns, in the types of emotion you bring to your work environment on a daily basis and how you express it. You spell it out in the way that you begin to communicate to your team and how you sow into them the vision you have of each individual's performance and how it will have an exponential effect when combined with the performance of the whole and how you are proud that they are with you. You spell it out by being the catalyst, by appealing to the self-interest of your team members, and by creating a synergy of relationship where people no longer merely come to a job, but where they come to a playing field, aspire to be one of the elite contributors, and where they fight for you wherever you may lead them.

This is the highest form of respect and honor. And when your team, your department, your organization sees you in this light; this is the ultimate form of Leadership.

Organizational Culture

Unity Of Purpose

The exact measure of an organization's promise and potential to be great resides in its ability to crank out innovative products and services. It is its ability to make customers or clients feel at ease and at home. The ability to project honesty, love, and care for its people and its surrounding community is a mark of a grand purpose. This purpose serves to unite all facets of the organization under one banner. It excites and inspires everyone to perform at their best, to be great so as to give the organization the best chance to fulfill its purpose. This purpose can be to serve other human beings in a service organization; it could be to eradicate poverty through education around the world. It could be to produce fun, safe products for children. Whatever the purpose is for your organization, it must be grand, it must provoke awe in the minds and bodies of the leadership first and then in each individual in every team. This purpose establishes a unity within the organization that primes the pump for growth and creativity. This purpose establishes a unity, a bond that can be felt by the outside world that your organization's reason for being is true to the heart. This type of purpose creates and draws support from the outside that assists, supports, and propels your marketing efforts. The first thing you must do, or at this moment that you must reestablish, is a unity of purpose.

The Power Center

The power that each individual feels when it comes to completing their task, performing at a high level, producing in a way that would make even the most demanding leader or owner proud, is a result of an environment that allows one to do so. The types of environmental attributes that allow for magnificent performance and those attributes that stifle the performance of the most willing participant are simple and obvious.

Are mistakes that are the result of attempts at creativity and innovation frowned upon? Are extra effort forced onto team members or is it a result of desired expression? Do you have to ask for the keys to the biggest and most grand effort of your team or is it freely given?

All of these answers are the result of the center of the organization, and whether it is strength based or weakness based; whether it is power based or fear based.

Many organizations, possibly yours, are led by individuals who still prescribe to the old traditional way of using the fear based authoritarian model of leadership, and thus the Power Center of the organization breeds decent, separation, low levels of effort, very little creativity, disrespect, and jealousy. This ultimately leads to poor customer service, poor relationships and conflict within the organization, poor performance and production.

A Power Center that is supportive, encouraging, and empowering to its individual team members to express themselves and be creative for the good of the organization, is a center that inspires growth. It allows for the development and the revealing of leaders rather than individuals simply looking to and/or waiting on a leader.

In short, a Power Center that allows members of the team to express themselves fully is a center that is on the brink of greatness. It is a center, an environment, which is on the brink of breaking through all perceived bounds. The limits of the organization are merely and precisely the result of the limits that the organization places on it people.

Free To Be Strong

The cleverest gimmick of all is the one that allows individual team members to be themselves.
In a society where it seems that many of the programs are designed to pacify and do everything for a person, versus, placing them in a position where they could grow and develop, similar to the caterpillar morphing into a magnificent butterfly.

16

A strong culture within an organization allows for individuals to be free. It does not bog them down with policy, guidelines, and protocols, especially ones that stifle growth, leadership, creativity, and initiative. If an organization is so rigid that individuals are not allowed or do not feel free to engage their work in a way that fully expresses who they are, then the organization is losing out on the most important and powerful part of its existence, and that is the immense resource located within each individual.

The strength of any organization is directly proportionate to the strength of its people. The solutions to all perceived challenges exist simultaneously. If you want to know how to provide greater quality products or services, ask your people. If you want to know what the customer or client's biggest concern is, ask your people. If you want to know how to make a product or a service better, ask your people. They already know the answers, the question is do they feel comfortable expressing themselves for the good of the organization. Do they feel free to be strong?

The Thread of Illusion

The common mistake is to think that our teams will take care of themselves. They will be polite. They will be encouraging and supportive. They will hold their performance, their production, and the level of customer service that they display as a high priority. They will put the organization's well-being and reputation before their own. Although these are noble thoughts for well-meaning people, it is still a mistake.

The mind of your team must be guided, for there are too many outside factors that affect a person's mindset, to leave the development and maintenance of a high performance mind to chance. Family life, sick parents, marriage, children, all other relationships, and financial issues can and do affect performance when they are carried into the work environment. With this being a fact, it is imperative that as a leader, you outline, sow, and model the necessary mental and emotional states to the level of performance and production that you desire within your team, your department and your organization as a whole.

Imagine, if you will, a bubble and inside it your team or your organization operates. Inside that bubble everyone performs supremely, powerfully, creatively. Inside that bubble, customer service is stellar. Inside that bubble, the camaraderie within the organization, the support and encouragement displayed between team members is remarkable. The entire organization, inside that bubble, is focused on the successful achievement of all of its highest goals and objectives, and all facets of every individual from their mental and emotional states, to their performance, to their production, to the realization of their limitless potential are in line with this end.

Outside of the bubble, life is happening, however, when the team pulls into your parking lot or walks onto your campus, mentally steps inside the bubble, there should be a mental shift to the attitudes and behaviors that are expected, and these attitudes and behaviors should/must be modeled and communicated consistently by you as the leader.

It is an illusion to expect otherwise.

The Basis Of Common Goals

If you have ever been an athlete or even participated in a sport or competition, the goal of winning served as the unifier of each individual's efforts. It unified thought patterns. It unified attitudes and emotions. It unified all behaviors in a specific direction, toward the highest possible efforts. It unified all behaviors into a vacuum solely restricted for behaviors and efforts that were conducive to the goal at hand, which was to win. The goal of winning also implied that a certain camaraderie between team mates was required. This chemistry is also necessary for the team to perform at its maximum, most efficient level. Dissent, incongruence and other related negative attitudes and emotions only serve to separate the team members, and stifles their ability to perform at a high level. This facet of team is often hoped for and often left unchecked, unmeasured, when its ramifications on the team are actually highly impactful and necessary to creating the synergy that really can push a team over the edge to a level of performance that is the result of motivation based on a feeling of obligation to team mates. A very powerful motivator.

The common goals within your organization serve the same purpose. They serve to unify your team into a specific direction. This direction requires specific states of mind, emotion and behavior to be successful and must be measured and evaluated to be sure that each individual is behaving, performing and producing at their highest level.

The common goals must be kept in front of the team, and must be described in a way that is inspiring. They must be stated in a way that creates and forces a unified whole, moving in the same direction, and does not allow for an environment of a multitude of fragments merely bumping into each other at the office, performing their job and waiting to get paid.

Distractions Dissolve Away

"Exactly what are we fighting for?" Interpersonal offenses and conflicts within an organization can often be solved by asking if they serve the highest purpose of the organization. Individual accomplishment and recognition can be a deterrent to performance when sought in lieu of the good of the whole.

It is the job of leadership to assist the team in seeing the success of individuals inside the success of the organization. It can't be forgotten that the human being seeks and yearns for growth and expansion, and that a position within an organization must provide it, or any single human being's stint will be short lived.

As a leader help your team members to grow. Help them to reach for greater heights in their development. Help them to expand to greater levels of possibility through responsibility, challenge, and the utilization of untapped creativity.

When team members feel that they are fully expressive, and engaged; when they feel as though they are truly contributing and being challenged beyond their previous capacity, there will be little room or time for interpersonal conflict with other team members to brew.

Can there be disagreements? Yes. However, they will be the result of attempts to drive the organization to new heights rather than for selfish personal gain or favor. There will also be attempts on the part of leadership to see and show how ideas and efforts can be meshed and integrated together for the good of the team and the organization.

The type of distractions that you may be used to, and believe to be normal, fall away when the individuals of the team feel engaged in growth and personal expression. It takes focus to tread uncharted waters. There is no time for dissention in the ranks if we are to survive.

Create this feel and this sense within your team and the distractions dissolve and fall away.

Trust To The Vision

In the end, any group, whether they be animals or human beings, adhere and trust to the vision. For animals, the vision is obvious; to survive. The animals must eat, they must protect themselves if need be, and hey, they even multiply and add to their force, their organization. There are specific duties required of certain segments of the group, hunting and things of that nature, and each animal is cared for, protected and supported for the benefit of the whole. To support and adhere to the vision.

The strength in your group, your organization is in your vision. If you own a hot dog stand your vision must be to provide the best hot dog and customer service experience ever. Otherwise you are just like everyone else.

As a leader and/or founder of your organization, you must trust in the vision. You must draw from the outcomes and not expect the impossible of people. The vision of the organization pulls and molds people. It shapes situations and circumstances from the inside out. It tugs at the hearts and minds of everyone associated, and as leadership you observe behaviors, and whether team members are in line with the vision that you have set forth and passionately proclaimed. Those that fail to align themselves with the vision will probably be better suited applying their talents somewhere else.

Trusting in the vision, and drawing only from the outcomes allows you a mental and emotional freedom to be calm and clear on the inside. It allows you to operate at full potential, to serve as the model of what personal individual effort in accordance to the vision should look like. As leadership, you must remember that the team is always, always, always modeling themselves and their behavior on what they see you do as leadership. So you must set the bar high for yourself if you want the bar of the team to be high.

The Go Ahead To Excel

There is a correct balance between policy and freedom that must be found. In most instances, policies are put in place in reaction to unwanted, unnecessary, unproductive behaviors. So to lay down the law, so to say, guidelines and rules are installed to make sure that employees act accordingly.

The funny thing is that when people are excited to be part of something, when they are excited about what they are trying to accomplish, you do not need to micromanage them. You do not have to make sure they come to work on time. You do not have to remind them to maintain high standards of quality.

Team members who are excited to be part of something, and are excited about what they are trying to accomplish show the utmost care for what they produce. They are masters of creativity and are highly sensitive to all facets of the organization that directly affects their products or services. Team members who are excited to be part of the team within your organization and who are excited about what they are trying to accomplish, stay late and come early. They do this on their own accord, not because they are asked or forced to.

So how do you find the balance between policy and freedom? How do you create the environment that gives your team members the go ahead to excel?

First, in your hiring process, you find people who are excited about being a part of the team and who are excited about what you are trying to accomplish.

Second, you allow them to self-govern. Once given the necessary guidance, direction and responsibility, allow them to engage their higher nature. Allow them to engage their creativity, all the inner and outer resources that they have available and that they have developed to perform their duties.

When you have created this type of environment and found the right people to work within it, you have a powerful team, a powerful organization that is going to fire on all cylinders, with many of the traditional challenges of organization being nonexistent.

Want to have the best restaurant? Hire good people. Want to have the best nonprofit? Hire good people. Want to have a school that produces students that excel? Hire good people. And once you have the people, be the extreme model and example of what the community, the team should look like while communicating and constantly reiterating and sowing the images of the vision of the organization, and then allow the team to go to work.

The behaviors, performance and production that you observe will alert you to whether things are on track. Only minor adjustments may be required.

Customer Experience

The Cover Is Not The Inside

Intentionally being the best that you can be has just a little more umph and power to it than pretending. To knock on the door of true service, the first step is to really mean it. I mean to your core, really mean it. The customer or the client who puts their trust in your company's services or products deserves no less. The truth is that customer service is more than the words that we speak and having the right answers. Customer service is the tone and attitude that you display whether in person, over the telephone, or over the internet in chat or email. The inner tone and attitude by which you go about your service to your customers or clients rings through in the words that you use and the mood or feel that is created during the interaction.

As a leader, what are the tones and attitudes that guide your level of customer service? And when we say customer service, we mean the service that we provide to customers or clients, and to colleagues, for when colleagues come to you for advice or support they are your customers as well.

What do you want the interactions to look like? What should they look like? At the highest level, "World Class," what does it look like? As a leader, this image must be the sole guide, and it must be sewn into each member of the team, to the point that it is unconscious and the only reference point for behavior when it comes to customer service. If this image is not the guide, then any emotion, attitude, or tone and the accompanying words that are a part of knee jerk automatic response to outside circumstances is possible, and that can be very detrimental to your business.

Customer service is a process whose power lies at the core of each individual. The surface smile, without the inner attitudes and conviction is not true, and your customers, your clients, your would-be loyal patrons know it. They can feel it.

25

Sow the image of the level of service that you wish to provide. Make it a priority so that the image gets burned, cemented into the unconscious of your team. Only then will it be the obvious choice, the only choice for behavior when it comes to the service to customers inside and outside of the organization.

The Image Of The Exchange – Conversation

The giving and receiving of information in your organization is a vital part, is the life blood of all that goes on. In the center circle we have the communication that goes on between colleagues and in the outer circle we have the communication that goes on between customers or clients. Both are of equal importance, because each is vital to the delivery of services and the development of relationship. Motivation and performance can be destroyed inside an organization by a two minute conversation. A customer can be won or lost in the same time frame.

What is the image of communication that you sow into your organization? Verbally, do you paint a picture to your team of what it should look like, and do you model that image to your team because you have gone on and become that picture, an example, before them.

The image of the exchange is critical. One of the worst factors within an organization that is most often left up to chance is human behavior, and it is simultaneously the very thing that impedes success. Team members having a bad day before they come on site, and disgruntled customers or clients who come in or call in with emotionally charged problems about a product or service are just a few of the things that can create the downward spiral in human behavior and motivation. A powerful image of what the communication should look like is vital to the maintaining of a mindset, of a standard that keeps your team and your organization in alignment with the successes and achievements that you seek.

Serving The Customer

There is no greater reward than to serve your customers; and your customers are not only those in positions to buy your product or service, but also your team members or colleagues within the organization.

There is no greater reward than to give of your knowledge, your skills, your care, your concern, or your highest intention when given the opportunity to serve. Too many alter their existence in a work/job situation because they feel as though they are strictly there to receive reward in the form of money, when the truth is that the reward is being put in a position to serve in an extreme capacity, and the money received is merely an exchange for the level of value and responsibility that they are able to accept and deliver.

It is a complete reversal of mindset, attitude and approach. The customers will have needs that extend far beyond the product or service that is delivered. They may need help understanding just how to integrate the product or service into their operation. They may need help seeing the benefit. Those customers that exist outside the organization will require care and understanding, and the more skilled you are at maintaining/choosing your mental and emotional state when in the midst of disagreement or confusion on the customer's part, the greater value you will be able to deliver.

Those customers/colleagues that you serve within the organization, at some point will also need your support, your encouragement, and anything else you can deliver to assist them in the performing of their duties. In these moments, it is also required that you exhibit the strength to choose the mental and emotional state by which you operate, to display a strength behind your service that is revered, respected, and looked up to.

To serve the customer, on both fronts, at its core requires you to choose who you want to be, should be, need to be, in order to be unforgettable/remarkable; and this requires holding the needs of the customer high and doing all you can to support and alleviate pain and confusion wherever it may be.

Serve your customers, inside and outside of the organization. Choose to be honorable in all of your professional encounters, and prove yourself worthy of their business and/or their gifts.

Empathy In The Highest

To be sure, to recognize and be aware of the feelings of your customers is a trait of the highest regard. In one sense, it puts you in the shoes of the customer, realizing the problems or pain that they are experiencing so that you can provide the necessary solutions. It allows you to meet them on an emotional level, so that they can feel that you are truly there to help.

This does not only end with those fantastic individuals looking to purchase your products or services, it also lends to your customers, or colleagues inside of the organization. As leaders, the more you are a true person, lending a hand both inside and outside of the organization, the higher quality performance you will get from your team because now they realize that you care about the person and not just what the person can do for you.

Cultivating the quality of empathy has far reaching implications, yet the results of these efforts may not be noticeable and measurable at the outset. It may take time for your customers or your team to recognize the genuine nature of your efforts. It may take time for your team members to become aware of the best way, through their performance, to show there level of appreciation, but it does come back in a way that is both powerful and beneficial to all.

Be genuine in your concern. Do what you are capable of doing, and what you should do, and time will tell the rewards.

I Am Here For You

One of the common mistakes of many leaders who have not learned to slow down and trust in the outcomes of a situation is not to be present when they are in the presence of their customers, and in this sense I am speaking of colleagues or coworkers. As a leader, your inner organization customers look to you for advice, support, even the recognition for a job well done, and there is no better way to fulfill this unspoken request than to be fully present when communicating with them. It demonstrates that you care, that you are interested in their position and their concerns. It demonstrates that you are accessible both mentally and physically, and your team can feel your presence.

If you have ever been in the presence of an individual, perhaps speaking to a child, and you could tell that his focus was on something else, then you know what I mean.

Be there for your customers inside of the organization. This doesn't mean allow them to take up unnecessary time with conversation that does not directly affect their performance or the team's achievement. It means letting your customers, your team know that when they need you that you are available for them, and that their voice is valuable and important. This goes a long way when developing rapport and camaraderie with those that you mean to lead. Without this level of relationship, the work environment is merely a shell of what it could be, and the effort to motivate becomes much more difficult.

A line from a once popular movie, from a son to his father was, "YOU FORGOT TO BE THERE!"

Be there for your team and they will reciprocate with effort and performance stemming from a motivation that far exceeds monetary reward; and that is what you want.

Destroying The Competition

The competition does not know what hit them when you have an entire organization in alignment with their purpose and their goals; when you have high quality individuals in an environment where they are supported, clear on the direction, clear on what their role is, and are free to maximize their talents and gifts for the good of the team.

When the seeds of greatness within each individual have been firmly planted and watered, nurtured, to the point that uninhibited growth are inevitable, that is when the power and potential of the organization is approaching critical mass, and the force of the collective is set to determine its own fate rather than it being determined by any outside efforts.

Compare this with an organization whose team is guided by fear based tactics, whose leadership is not in the business of supporting and encouraging their team members. This is an organization where the creativity and potential of its individual team members is stifled by rules, regulations, and micromanagement. Compare this to an organization whose purpose is not clearly stated, and whose team has no clear vision about the direction or their personal identity and worth within the organization. Compare this with an organization whose leadership puts people in place and then has very little communication with them, leaving the team members feeling as if they are on a deserted island, out of touch and unheard by their leadership to whom they look to for advice, support, and the occasional sign of approval.

The family unit, that is your team, requires certain dynamics to be in place, an environment that allows them to grow and perform at the highest level, and when these factors are not in place, you get lack luster performance with lack luster results. This ultimately yields a lack luster organization which does poorly in the marketplace.

Just a little time cultivating the right environment for the people in your organization to flourish, cultivating and allowing the inner gifts and talents within each individual to present themselves and support the organization, creates a powerful force with exponential ramifications when the collective is guided by purpose, vision, and specific goals.

The competition, well free-running horses are more powerful and produce a lot more energy than horses forced to move by a whip; the balance is staggering and profitable.

Sincerity In Your Voice

When speaking with your customers, whether it is your team, or prospects looking to purchase your product or service, there is power in your words. It is very important never to get caught in the "*just another customer*" vortex, where you become indifferent to the customer's excitement, that feeling they have, such as when a child is anxious to play with a new toy. They have questions, they have concerns, and if you are able to satisfy them they will happily buy, or perform in their position.

Customers can sense if there is care in your voice. They can sense if you are interested in their success. They can sense if you care whether they are having a good day. They can sense if you are sincere, just trying to make the sale or just trying to move them along so you can get back to what you were doing. It is your job as a leader to make sure that in those moments, the critical result that is your desired outcome is the main focus.

Cultivate an inner awareness and understanding of the outcomes you want. Train yourself mentally to be present when your customers inside or outside the organization need your attention, and be sure to care.

If you care, you will always come across as the person to come to, and your customers will remember.

Family/Best Friend Needing Help

A core misconception about customer service is approaching it from the idea that customers are out there and we, the organization, are in here. Imagine for a moment if your customers where family members whom you were introducing to a new concept or a new invention. How excited would you be? How passionate would you be about the prospects of your concept or invention being able to help or support your sister, your aunt or uncle, your mother or father in their daily lives or in their businesses?

Now, what if you as a leader approached your customer service in that manner, and taught your team to come from that place as well? There would never be a lack of energy. There would never be a lack of passion and conviction. There would never be a lack of true purpose, and those that you call customers would know it. They would feel it. It would be contagious like the energy of a sports competition that pulls you in.

All of this happens with change of mind, with a change in how we envision customer service. If we are trying to get customers or clients, we are approaching it the wrong way. If we are trying to get something from our team members, who are our customers as well, we are coming from the wrong place.

If your team is part of the family, you maintain a certain standard, a certain level of respect, concern and excellence. If your customers are a part of the family, you maintain a certain standard, a certain level of respect, concern and excellence.

This is what gains and supports the respect and concern from your customers inside and outside of your organization. This is what causes them to spread the word about the powerful things you are doing. This is what lets them and everyone else know that you care.

Trembling At The Thought

Incredible customer service is truly in the eye of the beholder. It is in the mind and heart of those who have had the privilege or the curse of having been in your presence, whether it was you as a leader in your organization, or your team in a colleague, vendor relationship, or a sales situation.

The trick is that you as an individual control the experience. You merely must remember the mental and emotional state that you were in the last time you had a fantastic interaction with anyone, and come from that place.

Entertain for a moment, the thought of speaking with a long lost best friend, or a favorite cousin during the holidays. What does that interaction look like? How does the warm embrace feel of engaging a loved one with care, joy and respect? The mere site of them sent energy racing through your body and brought a smile to your face. Remember, we are talking about the thought of this interaction, this meeting.

Now imagine carrying this image with you and simply replacing the face with that of your colleagues, your team members, your vendors and suppliers, your past, present, and prospective customers. What kind of experience would you give to those who came in contact with you? How would they feel about you? How would they describe you to other potential customers? How would your colleagues and team members feel about you after this experience? How long would they stay in the position if this was the experience they received from leadership? What type of effort would your team be willing to give for a leader who provided this type of experience?

A specific dimension of effects are associated with the business or organization that regularly experiences conflict, dissatisfaction of team members, and lack of respect between colleagues and team members, and it is definitely not high quality customer service, performance and creativity. These types of results are only associated with individuals who feel empowered, who are supported, who feel respected and heard, and feel as though they are taking some personal stake in the company.

As a leader, you have the ability to control the experience; you simply need to simulate the desired situation and experience in your mind. Once you have mastered this, it must be taught to your team. The stakes are high, and the experience is what is remembered both inside and outside of your organization. The experience generates performance both inside and outside of the organization, and as a leader, you are the catalyst.

Sales

Confidence In The Present, "Yes"

The making of a true sales champion is the confidence of and in the sale through and through. The energy of conviction and passion in a product or service is far more powerful than the skill to overcome objection and to be without it. In an era of freedom, social expression, and personal responsibility, individuals have the resources to gain all the information that they need about a product. You do not really need to bombard them with all the facts of your offering because nine times out of ten they have researched it already. What they lack is the conviction of which product out there is the best solution for them, and that requires passion, conviction and confidence. Often it requires personal experience with the product or service to really push a prospect over the edge. The ability to describe how a product or service has personally benefited you is a greater selling point and provides you with the ability to answer every question possible.

To whom do you owe the confidence of the sale? This is the initial question of them all. Nervousness and fear of any kind translates into distrusts and questionable performance, so this question must be addressed first. Confidence is a feeling, an inner knowing that is displayed, and if you have ever felt confident in your life, you can feel it now. No one can give it to you and no one can take it away. Simply remember a time you felt totally confident. Remember a specific time. See what you saw through your own eyes, hear what you heard, feel the feelings as if you were totally confident right now! This is how you can call forth any inner feeling to the present moment, and when you have it you must act.

This is required to perform all the tasks leading up to the sale. This is required to exude the inner knowing during the sale. This is what is required to perform the necessary follow up after the sale, to further the relationship, gather referrals, promote word of mouth and increase reputation.

The biggest mystery in sales has a subjective answer, and that answer lies in the expectation of "yes." The expectation of "yes" through and through has magnificent power. It draws the resources that you need. It pulls together the words to say. It filters the air and leads everyone involved to a certain predetermined point. The expectation of "yes," stumbled upon makes for a tool in processing new clients. The expectation of "yes," used consciously, is a guiding premise in networking, prospecting, and on sales calls.

Committing To Safety, "Yes"

One of the first major concerns of your client or customer is, "Do you have my best interest at heart?" The client wants to know this. They are already bombarded with sales pitch after sales pitch; advertising for every product imaginable. Do you care about them, their family, their company, their organization? This is not something you need to tell them, it is something they can feel. Do you commit to their well-being, their success, their purpose? These are the questions that your clients want answered first.

So who are you, and what do you stand for? Do you stand for the client and all ways that your product or service will benefit them or place them in the lead? Do you understand their position, their concerns, and the direction in which they are going? Do you understand the impact that a change in their current provider or the addition of a new service will have on their organization or on their family? Do you know the impact that investment in your product or service will have on their bottom line?

If in getting a "Yes," driving toward a "Yes," you have carefully considered all of the possible scenarios, the positives and the negatives for your client, and you are able to articulate that what you offer is to their benefit, your prospective customers will have heard and felt that you are committed to their safety, and "Yes" will be on the horizon.

Who Is The Buyer

The interest of the salesperson is best to be focused on one thing, "The Buyer." There is nothing else of greater importance. Who are they? Where are they? What do they want? What are they interested in? What is important to them? What is MOST important to them? What do they consider before they make a purchase? What MUST they consider before they make a purchase? How high up on their need meter is your offer? How deep into the depths of their concerns does your offer go?

As much as you can find out about "The Buyer," about their true motivation, the closer you align yourself with the sale.

You must be able to see into their world, see it through their eyes. You must be able to understand their needs and concerns, know what they are trying to accomplish in the short and the long term, and once you know this, truly decide whether what you offer is a good fit for them.

Who is "The Buyer?" "The Buyer" is someone who is placing their trust in you to fulfill a need, to deliver on a resource that will provide them with greater efficiency, the edge on the competition, or peace of mind.

Do you accept this responsibility? Do you deserve this responsibility?

"The Buyer" is sensitive to whether you care or not, and this makes a difference in the sale.

You must KNOW "The Buyer."

Imaging The Sale

To begin the sales process, the sale must be a forgone conclusion. You must see the sale, each beautiful exciting part, and feel the exhilaration of completion, everything being done for the good and the benefit of the buyer.

But what can you truly control? You can truly only control yourself in the process, your efforts, your thoughts, and the emotion with which you go about your daily activities and all of your sales calls.

A truly powerful practitioner has conditioned him/herself to only see the end result of their activities. They have envisioned the sale in its entirety, and they relish, bask in the feeling of powerful command and control of their lives, which they feel when the deal is successfully closed. They image the end of the month when they have successfully surpassed their sales goals and are celebrating the success. They envision the end of the year when they have successfully accomplished all of their yearly goals and are celebrating, basking in the success.

They envision the end of the story, the activities, the feelings, the emotions, and allow that to drive them, to pull them, to polarize them from the inside out to that end.

The truly powerful practitioner trains their mind to only consider the end that they desire and nothing more. This is what maximizes their efforts, maximizes the opportunities, maximizes their potential and causes them to exude the confidence and expectation necessary to draw, attract, and align themselves with the resources needed to accomplish their sales goals.

Benefits and Excitement

A true key to immaculate sales is the ability to clearly articulate the benefits that your product or service can provide to the customer/client. Whether you offer a product, a service, or an entertaining experience, you must know what is in it for the buyer. How will they be better off? What is it going to do for them? Will it be safe or will they be able to taste the edge? Will it make things smoother or will it shake things up a bit? Your potential buyer may not know for sure what they want, and if this is so, they definitely are not clear on how what you offer can help them achieve it. If you know what you offer, backwards and forwards, then you can work your way backwards to your ideal buyer, and once you work your way backwards through the challenges that are experienced by the buyer, then you will be able to explain how your offer pulls them up, out, or through those circumstances toward what they want to have happen or experience.

You must also be excited. Your buyer reaching their desired end must make you ecstatic; maybe even make your heart skip a beat because it is exhilarating. You must feel the surge coursing through you and convey that passion to your buyers. This is a major key to your sales success; before sales cycles and processes, before answering objectives, you must be excited about your offer and what you can provide to your customers/clients. This is the top and bottom line to your sales success.

The Feel Of The Sale

If you are not able to recognize when the attention and/or the energy of the buyer is waning, you probably will not be able to navigate your way through to that glorious end. You have made the calls. You have scheduled the appointment. You have rescheduled the appointment, and now you are on the appointment. You are sitting smack dab in front of the potential buyers. Can you hold their attention, their energy, their curiosity as to what is in it for them? Can you successfully pull them through to the close where they will thank you for your persistence and patience?

To do this you must be aware of the subtle signals and signs that indicate whether you have babbled too much, have not asked enough questions, or are merely boring the buyer to death, who is now just trying to be polite.

Things like eye contact, sitting erect, and attentiveness are indicators that your buyer is engaged. They are interested in your offer, and are possibly already contemplating how to implement it to fulfill their needs.

Wondering eyes, that blank stare, or a predisposition toward other things may be an indicator that you have lost this buyer mentally, or that he may just have other issues at present that are dominating his thoughts.

Whatever the case may be, you must be aware, ready, and willing to grab that attention back if need be. This is the only shot at the sale you have.

You must be in constant search of, and maintain the correct feel of the sale. The feel of the sale is that energetic match between you, the buyer, and your product or service. Allow your desired end result to be the guiding light to all your words and behaviors, and convey that energy to the buyer. If you do this, the feel of the sale will appear.

Answering Questions - The Language Of The Sale

Distancing yourself from the normal mistake of merely discussing the features (bells and whistles) of your product or service is a first step in claiming sales superiority. What does the buyer want and need should be the main focus, the guiding question. Get to know them either through research or personal contact. What are their fears? What are their desires? What keeps them up at night?

If you can find the answer to these questions, you will find the language of the sale. The language of the sale being a narrow focus on the touching points of the buyer, a focus on those points for which the buyer gets emotional. It could be the best tasting hot dog. It could be the printer of all printers. It could be the absolute best care for your pet while you are away.
Focus on that which makes the buyer visibly excited, or relaxed, and the language of the sale will carry you to your desired location.

It is not enough to have a great product or service. It may not be enough to connect emotionally with the buyer, but if you do not connect, the missed sale will be a foregone conclusion.

Conclusion

All revenue producing activities, the performance of your teams, the experiences of your customers or clients, and the ability of your Leaders to lead, are all functions of a mind that is set on its Ideal experience. The practitioner who remains focused, from the inside out, on the circumstances that they want to experience, and aligns himself through thought, emotion, word, and behavior toward that end, becomes an unstoppable force moving swiftly toward completion and achievement. The practitioner engages the energies of the universe through the power of their own being to command and relentlessly expect success in their area of focus.

So which do you choose? As an obvious Leader, if reading this book, you have a choice. The choice is whether merely continuing to react when it comes to your daily activities, leaving success, opportunity, and reputation up to chance, or learn to command that which is the only place you are able to control, the mind, and begin to craft and carve out your vision for yourself, your team, and your company or organization from the inside out.

Long has the mystery been held close by a few, but now you have the opportunity to know and experience the truth and power that is latent inside of you and your team once you engage and begin to operate and perform from the inside out.

If we can be of service in any way, we are here for you.

About Benny

In Spirit I Thrive, In Mind I Fall. It Is My Job, To Unify Them All.

I now realize that for 2 decades I have been striving to release the true, authentic me that had been covered by fear based ideas and perceptions. (Get Past Yourself)

I am realizing that the life I once lived, and the life story that is being lived around me by family and friends is not a chosen life, but one that has been passed along. With elements of fear at its base; loss, pain, failure, and the embarrassment of mistake once defined me, now they propel me. (The Other Side Of Fear)

Now I strive to allow the true authentic, Source inspired me to breathe through at every moment. This grants me the knowing that my desires are pure and in line with the path that is specifically for me. (Allowing Me)

I did not need a teacher, a preacher, or a guru. All I needed was some Guidance and some Direction. (My Only Need)

And so it is with you!!

Benny

Leadership ~ Organizational Culture ~ Customer Experience ~ Sales

"Maximizing Human Performance and Potential By Commanding the Mind"

Question: What is the most important part of an organization?
Answer: The individual

Question: Do processes exist and operate prior to skill and behavior?
Answer: Yes.

Question: What are the lost/forgotten determinants to performance?
Answer: Inner workings of the mind.

Question: What do these processes consist of?
Answer: Images/pictures, sounds, feelings, tastes, smells, and self-talk.

Question: What is the most powerful choice?
Answer: A singular focus on desired outcomes with only consideration for their success.

Question: What is the result of this extreme focus?
Answer: Attraction of needed resources, acquire necessary skills; revealed inner blocks, revealed limiting ideas and beliefs that you hold about yourself, others, and what is possible.

Question: Do I influence my life experiences and the successful completion or accomplishment of my highest goals and objectives?
Answer: Yes, all experiences are greatly influenced by their human participants

Question: Who is most influential?
Answer: The person who is most congruent or in alignment with their desired outcome.

Question: Does the experience and performance of an organization have a determinant?

Answer: Yes, the cumulative mind and expectation of the whole.

Question: Can the cumulative mind of an organization be controlled?

Answer: Yes, the continuous modeling and communication of the organization's purpose and vision by its Leadership, coupled with the continuous sowing of the images, in the team, of the behaviors and types of performance that yield the desired results.

The Strategy Of Brilliance
M – Master Senses ~ E – Establish Ideal ~ P – Purify Mind

What You Learn, What You Gain:

- Learn to create ideals in and around your life, that dictate who you choose to be and how you perform;

- Understand, become aware, and experience the processes at work within each human being that dictate behavior and performance;

- Ability to dictate how you respond and behave in all situations;

- Ability to program desired outcomes, and remain in alignment with them from the inside out;

- Ability to identify limiting beliefs and emotions associated with undesired experiences;

- Ability to call upon prepared and pre-designed images that propel you into powerful mental and emotional states;

- Release of stress, doubt, worry and fear;

- Commanding presence and influence within your organization and abroad;

- Heightened awareness to solutions;

- Heightened creativity.

* Each individual mind, crystallized around ideal experiences and results, accompanied with the necessary guiding ideas and

beliefs, dictates the behaviors necessary for powerful performance.

* Increased profits, exceptional customer service, and a powerful work environment are staples of an organization operating with The Strategy Of Brilliance.

About The Ferguson Company:

The Ferguson Company is emerging as a world leader in reminding human beings of their limitless power and potential.

Whether in an individual setting, as a business, or the grand operation of a large organization, the mind of the individual is the fundamental starting point to all behaviors and all experiences. **The inner workings of the mind are the Points of Power.**

Alignment is the lost consideration. In approaching desired outcomes, goals, and objectives, is the mind solely focused, through and through, on that end? Are the thoughts, emotions, words and behaviors of each individual involved in sync, in alignment with that end?

It is possible to cancel the clutter, release all limiting beliefs and ideas, and cultivate an inner, laser like focus that produces a level of performance that will not be denied. It is possible to claim results and outcomes before they appear in outer physical experience.

These are all forgotten attributes of the human being.

The Strategy Of Brilliance is a guiding premise, with three comprehensive operatives:

M – Master Senses
Recognize that all outer, physical experiences are effects and not causes. Therefore all less than desirable outcomes are no longer looked at as failure, but feedback. This feedback warrants inner adjustment, until the behaviors and performance that is displayed yields the desired outcomes.

E – Establish Ideals
Generate images of the most desired outcomes or experiences.
Create these images in their most perfect form, engaging all of the
senses.

P – Purify the Mind
Begin process of installing powerful, driving ideas and beliefs, while
simultaneously becoming aware of and replacing all limiting ideas,
beliefs and emotional blocks that are already present within the
mind.

Whether improved individual performance is desired, or the
complete overhaul of an organization, *The Strategy Of Brilliance*
addresses the core foundation to behavior, performance and
experience. *The Strategy Of Brilliance* addresses mindset, the only
area of a human being that precedes skill.

If you or your organization is truly ready to realize your limitless
power and potential, then you must learn to master the mind.

Connecting With Benny:

Facebook: www.facebook.com/bennyrfergusonjr

Youtube: www.youtube.com/BennyFergusonJr/videos

Twitter: www.twitter.com/BennyRFergusonJ

Contacting Benny:

Initial contacts to Benny for discussions, interviews, one – on - one or group coaching, speaking or training may be made through telephone or email.

Phone: 336-546-7142

Email: BennyFerguson@TheFergusonCompany.com

www.ingramcontent.com/pod-product-compliance
Lightning Source LLC
Chambersburg PA
CBHW070916210326

41521CB00010B/2204